# GECKO TAILS

## COMPOSED BY
## SYLVIA WOODS

COMPANION CD ENCLOSED

# Table of Contents

### A Few Notes from Sylvia Woods:

#1. Fingering preferences are very personal. My fingerings will give you a guideline from which to start. Feel free to change any of them. It won't hurt my feelings at all!

#2. These pieces can be played on either a lever or a pedal harp. Lever harp players should set their levers as indicated at the beginning of each piece. There are no lever changes within any of the pieces. Pedal harpists will have pedal changes in "Sticky Toes."

#3. If you have your lever harp tuned to 3 flats, play "The Gecko Stroll" version on page 30. Everyone else should play the version on page 28.

#4. The lowest note in any of these pieces is the G that is 10 strings below middle C. "The Gecko Stroll" on page 28 can be played on a harp with just one octave below middle C.

#5. The metronome markings are guidelines to give you an idea about the approximate tempos that I play them. However, none of the pieces should be played "metronomically."

#6. Have fun and enjoy!

With many thanks to Paul Baker and Denise Grupp for their editing assistance.

Thanks also to Paul Baker, Rachel Jones, Therese Lopez, Aedan MacDonnell, ShruDeLi Ownbey, and Heidi Spiegel for help with the titles.

And, to all the geckos who live with me in Kauai: mahalo for your inspiration!

Cover artwork © by David Kolacny
CD recorded at TV Juice Productions, Kilauea, Kauai, Hawaii

ISBN 0-936661-35-6

# Fun Gecko Facts

Geckos are the only lizards that can produce sounds. Their name comes from the clicking or chirping "geck-o" sound made by some species.

There are over 900 species of geckos worldwide living on every continent except Antarctica. Eight species live in Hawaii. The most common geckos on the island of Kauai are House Geckos, Mourning Geckos, and Stump-toed Geckos. Adults range from about 3" to 5fi" long.

Geckos live in lots of the houses of Hawaii. They are considered by many to be good luck. They often stake out territories; there might be a front window gecko, a kitchen sink gecko, a picture frame gecko, etc.

One good reason to have geckos in your house is because they are carnivorous. They can eat four to five mosquitoes or termites a minute. They also eat cockroaches, crickets, and ants.

When a gecko is caught by its tail, it releases the tail, which twitches for a while and allows the gecko to escape capture. The gecko will later grow another tail.

Geckos have immovable eyelids; their eyes are always open. They lick them to keep them clean.

# Sticky Toes

A gecko can dash up a smoothly polished glass surface, sticking and unsticking its feet 15 times a second. It can hang from a ceiling, if it wants to, by a single toe. Even in a laboratory-created vacuum, where suction would do little good, a gecko's foot will still stick. How does it do it?

In the year 2000, scientists from Lewis and Clark College, the University of California, and Stanford University published results from their studies of Tokay Gekos, the largest geckos on the planet. Each gecko toe has a network of about 2 million tiny hairs called setae, each about a tenth the diameter of a human hair. One seta can lift the weight of an ant. A million setae, which could easily fit onto the area of a dime, could lift a 45-pound child and a gecko using all of its setae at the same time could support 280 pounds.

The end of each seta is further subdivided into hundreds to thousands of structures called spatulae. These tiny pads work through the weak attraction that molecules have for one another when they are brought very, very close together, called "van der Waal's forces." This force is what allows the gecko to stick to virtually any surface -- even polished glass.

As one researcher said: "Geckos have developed an amazing way of walking that rolls these hairs onto the surface, and then peels them off again, just like tape. But it's better than tape." Scientists are hoping that this knowledge will help them invent a gecko-inspired adhesive that is dry, self-cleaning, and reusable. It could be used on semi-conductors, robots, and a variety of consumer products. Who knows, maybe someday we'll all be able to climb walls and ceilings like Spiderman (or like geckos!) with special gecko gloves and shoes.

# Sticky Toes

by Sylvia Woods

This piece is a hornpipe. The dotted notes should not be held as long as written.
It should "swing," with ♩.♪ played as ♪³♪

Lever harp players: set middle C# before you begin. It will not change throughout the piece.

♩ =120 - 125

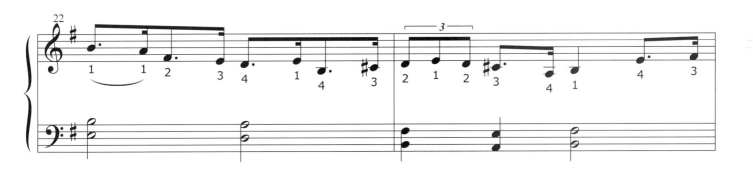

# View from the Ceiling

by Sylvia Woods

In the left hand of the first 34 measures, up until the first 12/8 bar, muffle the G by replacing your 2nd finger on the G as you play the A.

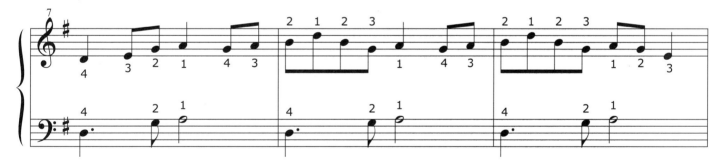

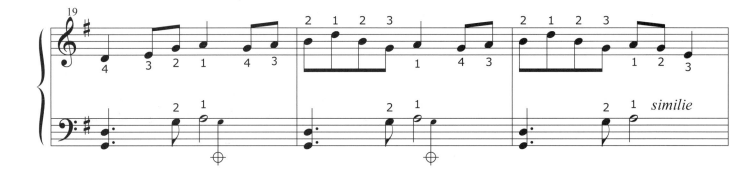

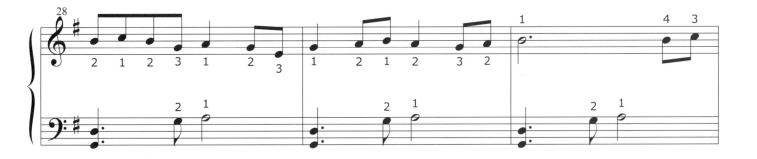

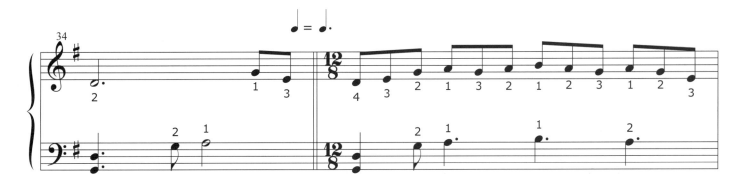

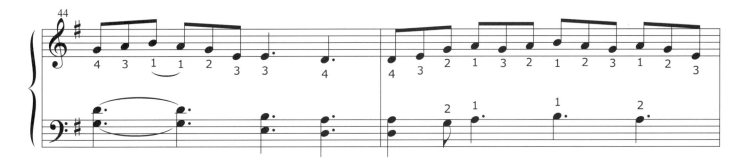

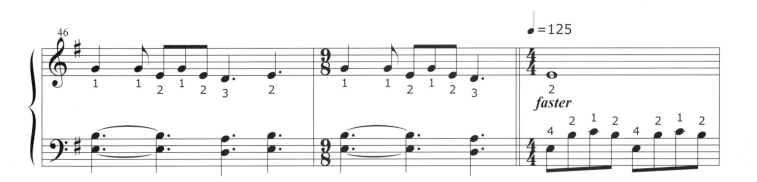

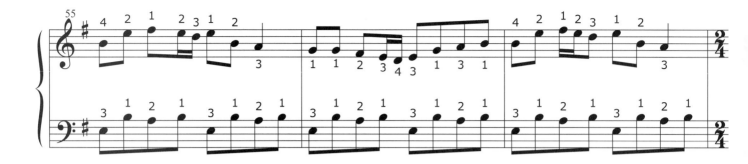

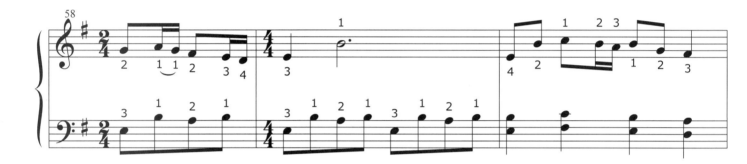

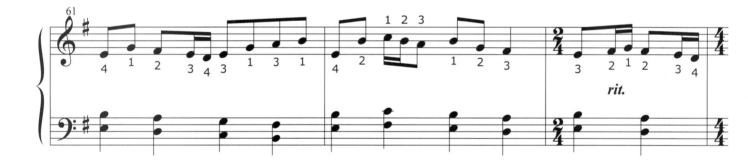

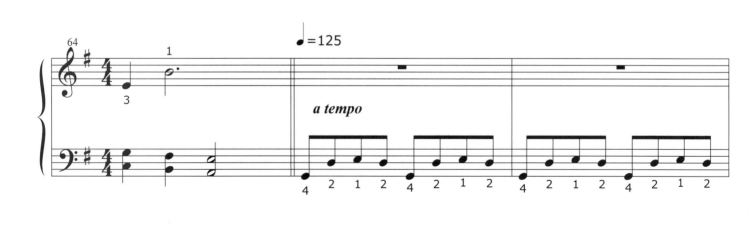

**13**

# Dancing in the Waterfalls

by Sylvia Woods

Intro slow and dreamy

Crisply ♩.=110 - 115

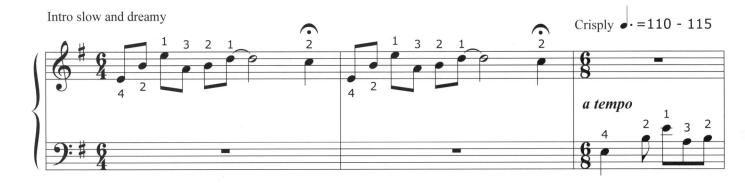

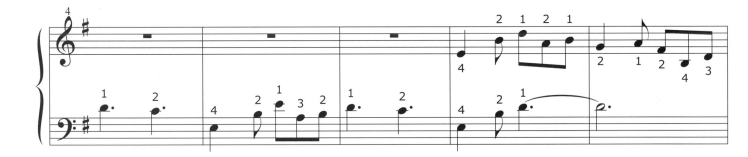

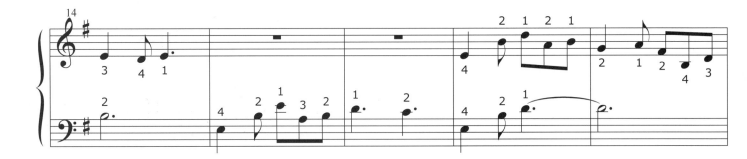

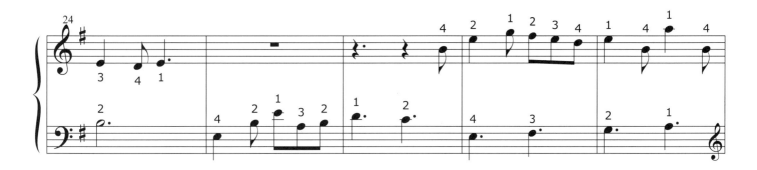

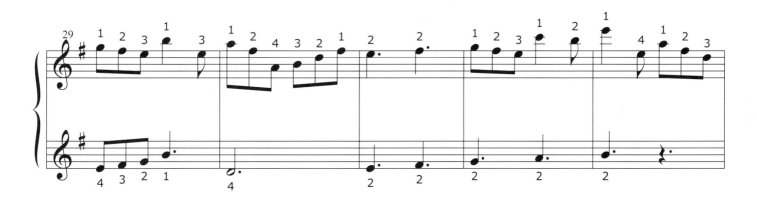

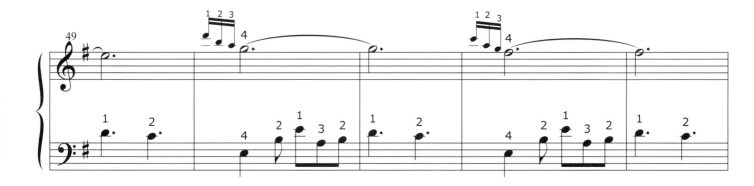

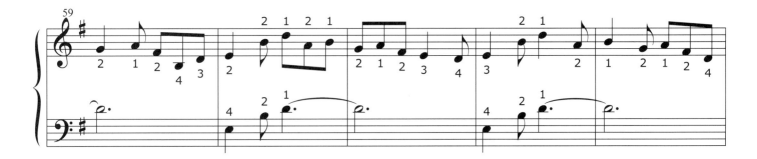

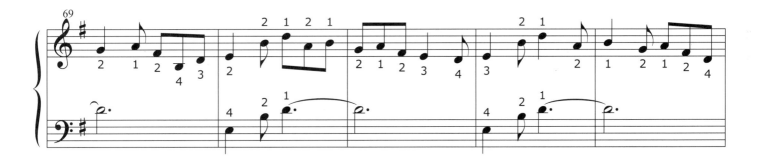

**19**

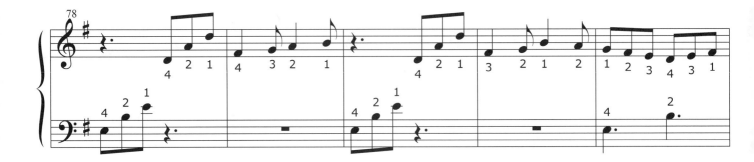

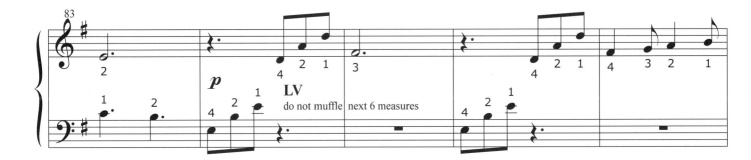

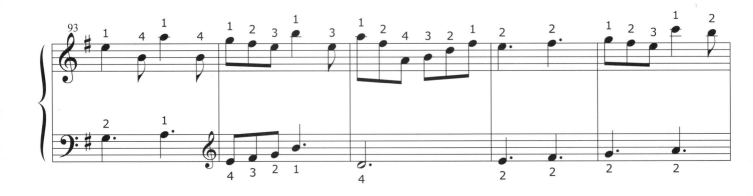

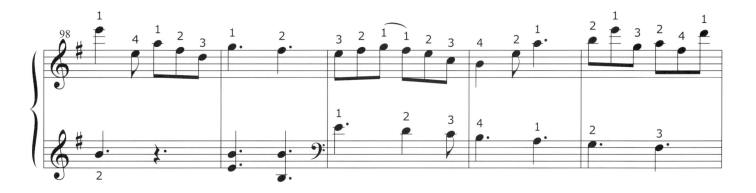

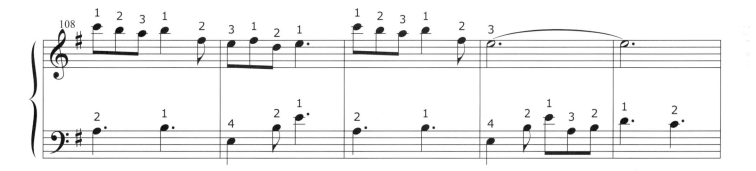

# Tropical Dreams

by Sylvia Woods

There are only a few left-hand patterns in this piece.  Once you learn them, you won't have to worry about reading the ledger lines.  So take a few minutes to acquaint yourself with these patterns, and memorize them. The left hand in measure 1 is repeated through measure 11.

Measure 28 extends this pattern 2 notes higher.  Measure 29 extends it another 2 notes, through measure 41. The original pattern repeats itself up a 5th (beginning on E) in measures 57 to the end.

Here are the patterns, written using both clefs to help you learn them.  Play all the notes with your <u>left</u> hand.

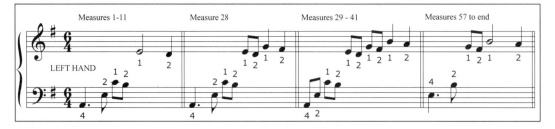

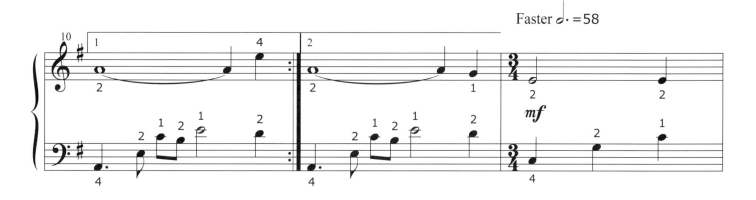

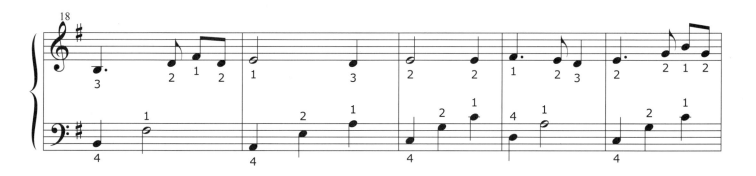

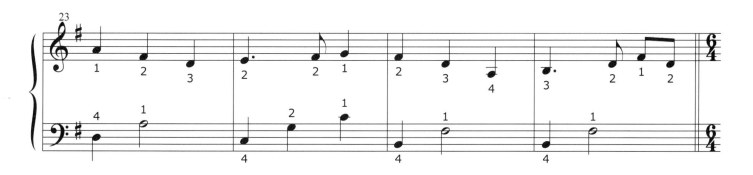

Slower ♩=110

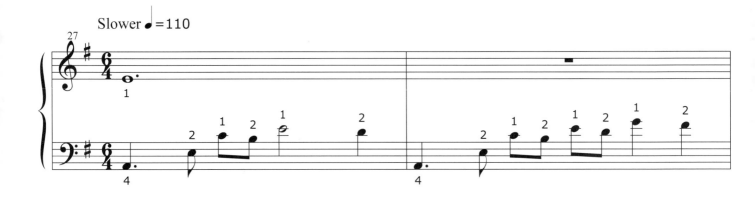

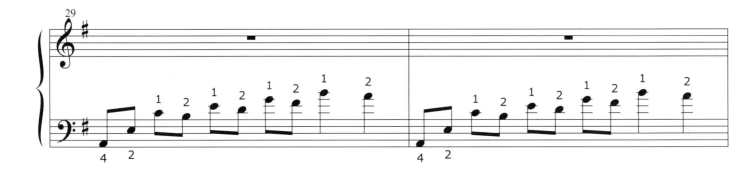

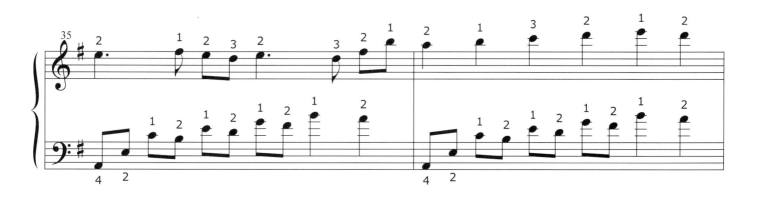

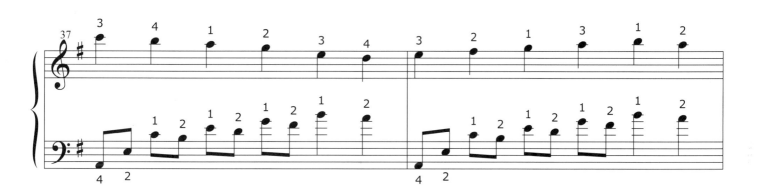

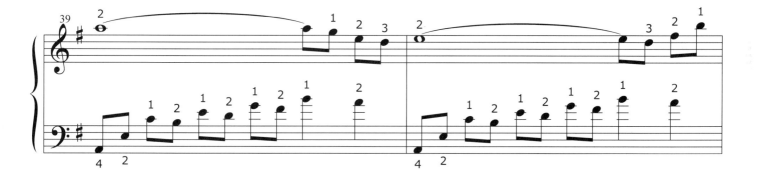

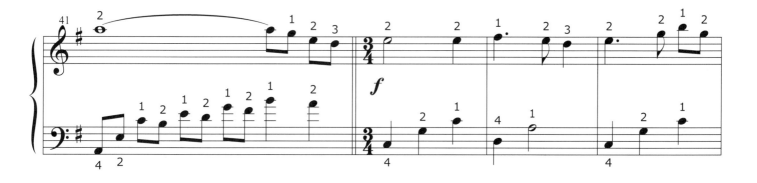

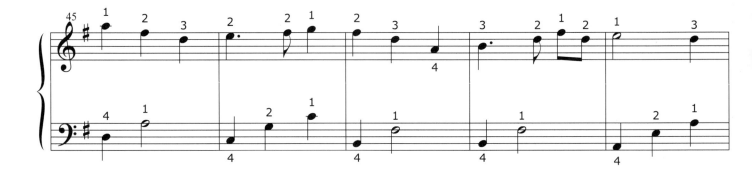

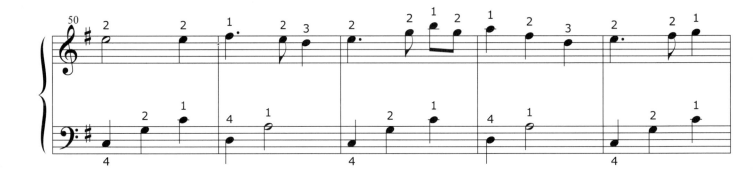

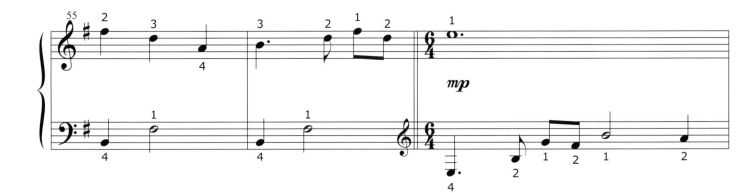

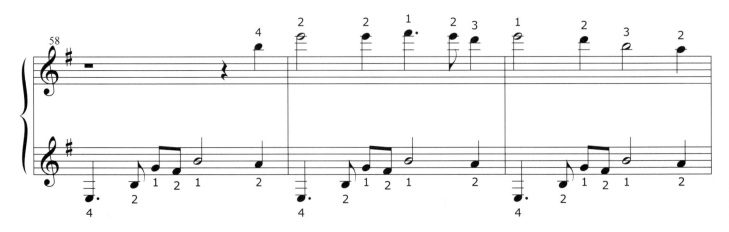

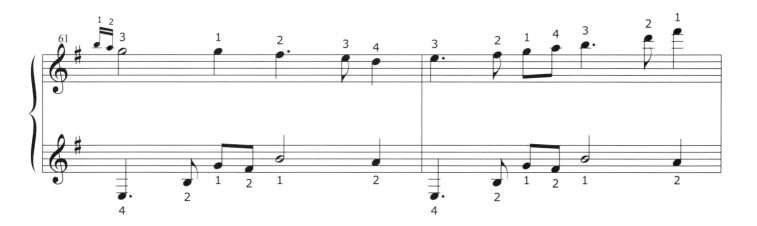

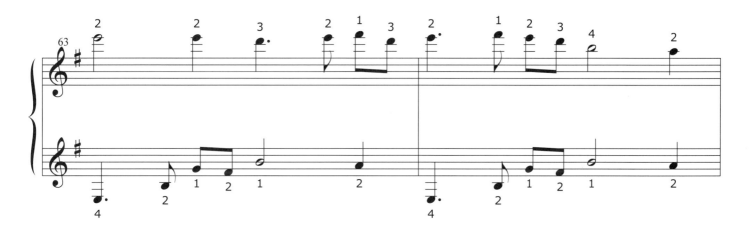

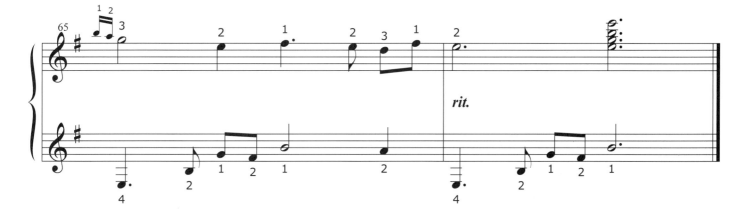

# The Gecko Stroll

by Sylvia Woods

This arrangement is for lever harps tuned to the key of C, and for pedal harps.
Sharp all your E's before you begin. These will not change throughout the piece.

Playfully ♩=90

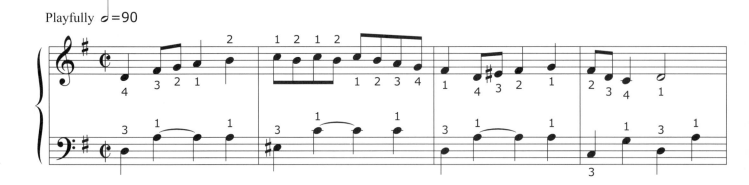

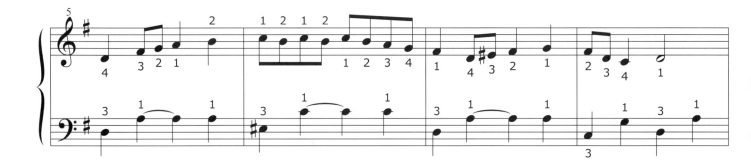

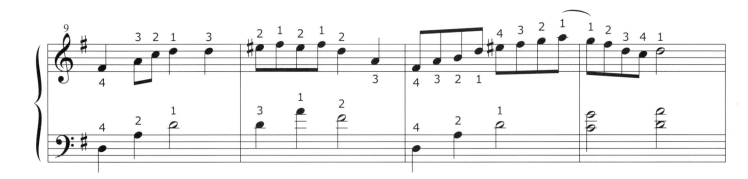

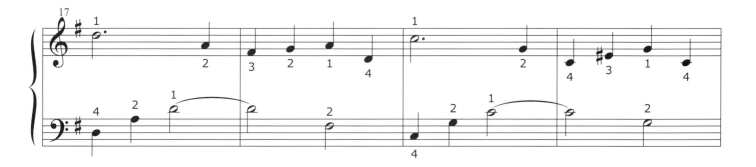

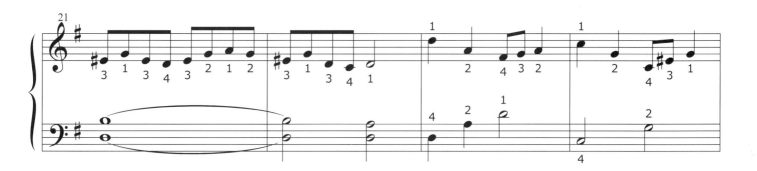

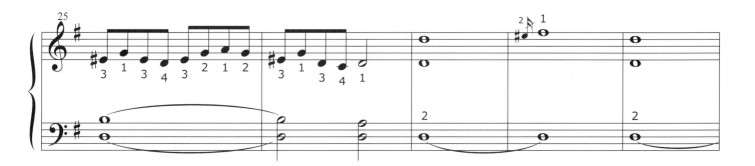

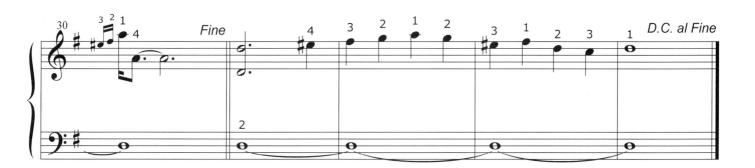

**29**

# The Gecko Stroll

by Sylvia Woods

This arrangement is for lever harps tuned to 3 flats.
Sharp all your D's before you begin.  These will not change throughout the piece.

Playfully ♩=90

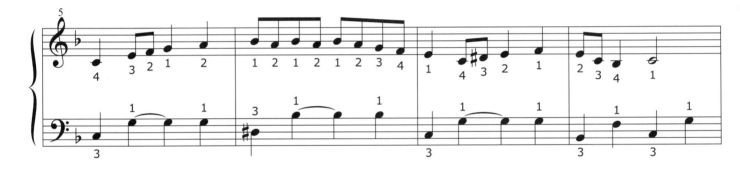

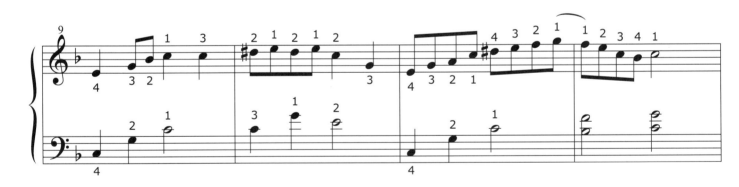

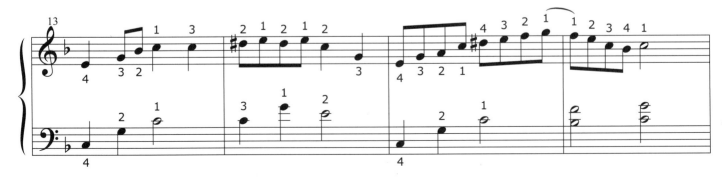

**30**

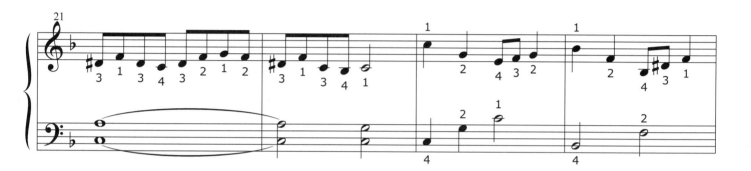

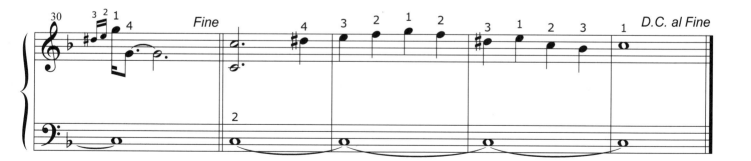

# Other Books by Sylvia Woods

Music Theory And Arranging Techniques For Folk Harps

John Denver Love Songs Arranged for Harp

Hymns And Wedding Music For All Harps

Teach Yourself To Play The Folk Harp

Lennon and McCartney for the Harp

Andrew Lloyd Webber for the Harp

50 Christmas Carols For All Harps

40 O'Carolan Tunes For All Harps

Irish Dance Tunes For All Harps

52 Scottish Songs For All Harps

50 Irish Melodies For The Harp

Chanukah Music For All Harps

76 Disney Songs For The Harp

Jesu, Joy Of Man's Desiring

The Harp Of Brandiswhiere

Beauty And The Beast

Andrew Lloyd Webber

4 Holiday Favorites

22 Romantic Songs

Pachelbel's Canon

Songs of the Harp

The Wizard of Oz

# Sheet Music by Sylvia Woods

Simple Gifts

Winter Bells

Wondrous Love

America Medley

Spiritual Medley

Dead Poets Society

The Water is Wide

2 Christmas Medleys

In the Bleak Midwinter

All the Pretty Little Horses

House at Pooh Corner / Return to Pooh Corner

Love Theme from the Titanic: My Heart Will Go On

If you would like to receive a **free catalog** of music by Sylvia Woods
and other books, recordings, harps, and accessories, please write to:

**Sylvia Woods Harp Center, P.O. Box 816, Montrose, CA 91021 USA**

**You can also find us on the Internet at www.harpcenter.com**